Open Hearts,
Helping Hands

Open Hearts, Helping Hands

Prayers by Lay Volunteers in Mission

Compiled by Carl Koch, FSC, and Michael Culligan

Saint Mary's Press
Christian Brothers Publications
Winona, Minnesota

The publishing team included Carl Koch, FSC, development editor; Rebecca Fairbank, copy editor; Gary J. Boisvert, production editor and typesetter; McCormick Creative, cover designer; pre-press, printing, and binding by the graphics division of Saint Mary's Press.

The acknowledgments continue on page 94.

Printed in the United States of America

Printing: 6 5 4 3 2 1

Year: 1999 98 97 96 95 94 93

ISBN 0-88489-289-1

People like Angelica and Sara
are touching me profoundly with their lives—
their simplicity, questioning, and service to others
amid the illness, poverty, and at times
desperate situations of their own lives.

I am learning a deeper sense of humility.
Be assured, however, that I am happy here—
thankful for the gift of life and the opportunity
    to be living the struggles and challenges
with the people in La Faena.

Anne Attea
Holy Cross Associates Volunteer Program

Contents

Preface

One of the many fruits of renewal in the Christian church has been the dynamic development of lay ministry through volunteer programs. Lay volunteers serve humankind in their home countries and in other lands, and they provide the church with a rich resource in spirituality.

This book of prayers and reflections displays the wonderfully diverse, profound, and invigorating lives of faith, hope, and love that lay volunteers in mission experience. It is hoped that the prayers will inspire, instruct, and move you, whether you are a lay volunteer or not. The prayers touch on themes and feelings at the heart of ministry: experiencing God's call; making adjustments in new settings; being touched by the lives of poor people; working with children, teens at risk, or battered women; living in community; and giving thanks. The prayers are honest and articulate, and they reflect the depth of insight that often comes as a gift from ministry.

The volunteers who contributed prayers and reflections come from the United States and Canada. Many of the over one hundred existing North American lay volunteer or missionary programs are represented in this book.

How *Open Hearts, Helping Hands* Came to Be

The idea for doing this book came about while Mike Culligan and I were washing dishes one night after supper. Mike had come to interview prospective volunteers at Saint Mary's College in Winona, Minnesota, and he was staying at our community house. Because Mike knew that I edited and wrote books on prayer and spirituality, he asked if I knew of any books that volunteers could use for community prayer. He wanted prayers that spoke to the particular experience of laypeople in service or ministry. I could not recall ever seeing such a book.

As we talked further, both of us became enthused with the notion of putting together such a book. We knew that many of the thousands of volunteers had written journal entries, poems, reflections, or prayers over the years. Thus, we decided to invite lay volunteers in mission to submit their writings so that we could assemble them into a book of prayers and reflections.

Over several months, Mike and I circulated notices about the project to directors of volunteer programs, and we had the invitation for submissions published in newsletters commonly read by present and former volunteers. Many of the program directors gave their enthusiastic support to the project.

By 1 March 1992, Mike and I had received a hefty stack of prayers, poems, articles, reflections, and even a song or two. Then we began reading, sorting, and selecting. As we worked, we developed a format for the book. Some of the long submissions were excerpted for use in the prayers, but four of them were included by themselves as reflections (see prayers 20–23); we just did not have the heart to shorten these four stories.

Naturally, the worst aspect of editing the book was having to eliminate some of the submissions. We just did not have space for all of the wonderful work.

Praying Our Experiences

In his book *Praying Our Experiences,* Joseph F. Schmidt offers this helpful insight:

> *Praying our experiences* is the practice of reflecting on and entering honestly into our everyday experiences in order to become aware of God's word in them and to offer ourselves through them to God. . . .
>
> We pray our experiences when we use the content of our lived existence as the content of our prayer. (P. 9)

The prayers and reflections in this book are composed of stories about the experiences of lay volunteers in mission. Indeed, most of the submissions were not written as prayers. As a result, they may have a slightly unfamiliar sound to them.

However, when we allow ourselves to resonate and empathize with the stories, and when we bring our own similar experiences to the stories, they become genuine offerings to God. For example, when reading the humorous psalm in prayer 15 about learning to communicate, we can allow ourselves to enjoy the humor, offer it to God, and let the wisdom of the psalm-story touch our own memories of similar unsuccessful communication attempts.

Prayers like these offer us new experiences with which to pray. As we recite and reflect on them, we are praying—that is, we are interacting with the loving God who dwells with us, in us, and all around us. At the same time, we are hearing the word of God in new ways.

Using the Prayers

Whether you use the prayers alone or with a group, try to create a prayerful mood with candles, an open Bible, or a crucifix. If a quiet place is not available, know that a loving God is present everywhere.

Begin by silently recalling God's presence. If you feel restless or rushed, spend some moments simply relaxing your body—letting go of all the tensions of the day, all the time demands, all your projects. Breathe deeply and slowly. A period of meditative breathing in God's presence is a prayer of simple attention. If you find it helpful, repeat a short prayer-phrase in harmony with your breathing. For example, "You are present, Holy Friend." When you are present to God, engage in the rest of the prayer.

Pray each of the sections carefully, letting the meaning of the words take form for you. Each word and phrase is an offering to God. Give your offering deliberately. Pause in silence between each section. Go slowly—very slowly.

The prayers may be freely adapted to meet your needs. For instance, you may want to add a song at the start or end of a prayer. Other suggestions follow.

The opening prayer, psalm, hymn, and closing prayer in each section may be used in a variety of ways by a community. For instance, you may wish to have one person read the opening and closing prayers. The psalm may be recited with two groups alternating stanzas. The hymn may be recited in unison or by rotation—each member of the group reciting one or two lines. You may want to share reflections or petitions after either the reading or the hymn. Vary the way in which the prayers are offered, while being sure to include everyone in the prayers.

A Final Word of Thanks

Great thanks are due to all the lay volunteers in mission who submitted their prayers and reflections for this book.

Thanks also go to all the directors of volunteer programs who announced the project and encouraged submissions. Your cooperation made the book possible.

Mike and I are confident that all of you who pray these prayers will find consolation, inspiration, and great hope.

Carl Koch, FSC

1

Call

Opening

You call us, God, in unique ways to our own way of service. May we always be open to your call, knowing that it leads to love, and thus to you. Speak, loving God, we are listening.

Psalm

We make up a candle together.
I am the wick,
surrounded by the candle wax of God's love,
ignited by the match, Jesus,
who lights me with the flame of the Holy Spirit,
to form the light of Christ,
and give forth life.

Without the fuel of this loving candle wax,
I would light up instantly and then extinguish myself.
I want to burn instantly,
but I know the more wax I have surrounding me,
the more my light will shine.

But I cannot be an instantly fat candle, either.
The Candle Maker cannot dip me in the candle wax
for me to instantly have an inch or two of wax
    blanketing me.
It takes time.

First, the Candle Maker must dip me in the candle wax,
and let me dry.

When the Candle Maker thinks I am ready—
not when I, a mere wick, think I am ready—
only then will I be dipped for another coating of loving
    candle wax.

How long a process . . .
but how patient is the Candle Maker . . .
so much more than I,
who felt ready to burn as a mere wick . . .
how wise.

The Candle Maker knows
the more candle wax gradually thickened on me,
the less tendency I will have to break, or to chip.

The more candle wax solidly encircling me,
the more I can handle the nicks and chips;
the less they will matter.

It gives me comfort to know that should I break,
I can easily be repaired by just one more dip
    in the candle wax. . . .

And, throughout all this,
how remarkable—
the light of Jesus Christ cannot shine without the wick,
me,
else the loving candle wax of God just sits,
patiently,
waiting for a wick to fuel. . . .

Abba, love me, teach me to be patient with your ways,
to realize and have faith
that you are constantly dipping me
in your candle wax of love
to make me strong, bright, and enduring—
and in your time, not mine.

Megan Reilly
Los Angeles Volunteer

Reading

I came to India so I could love God. I wanted to work with the poor, work hard, and live a simple life. I felt like India was where God wanted me to be. But what have I always done with my life? Counseling women and children, loving my family and friends, watching the stars, going for a drive through the Texas hill country, nursing a stray puppy back to health, or baking brownies for my landlord. I can love God in my every day, wherever I am, whatever I am doing. I feel like the way I live my life is my prayer, and loving God is what I've been doing all along.

I am here in India, and I have been loving God. The last two months I've been caring for abandoned babies and children with the Missionaries of Charity in Jamshedpur. Changing the diaper of an unwanted child. First one, then two, three. Changing ten diapers in ten minutes. Feeding the little boy whose mother died when he was born, if only he could sit still then this rice and dal wouldn't be all over his face. My favorite little girl, one of many abandoned girl babies in India, wiping her nose for the twelfth time one morning because of the chronic cold she's had for over a month. Learning more about unconditional love.

I am here in India, and I think I've been loving God. Working with the poor. In the last two months, four babies have died and one is blind because of poor nutrition and disease. Working hard. Standing on my feet much of the day, sitting on the hard floor the rest of the day, catching colds and lice from the children, and changing all of those diapers when all I really feel like doing is taking a nap. Living a simple life. Riding a bicycle to work each day as I dodge cows, goats, pedestrians and trucks, learning what it's like to not always have electricity or hot water, taking baths from a bucket.

I am here in India, and is this really loving God? Did I want to see extreme poverty, people dying in the streets, and did I want to see despair? "People in the world, wherever we are, we're all basically the same, you know," an Indian friend tells me after knowing him for fifteen minutes. What words of wisdom and how true. My loving God and service here isn't going to make any big difference. Indian lives were going on before I came and will continue long after I am gone.

I came to India because I thought that this was how I could love God. I knew India was a right thing, but my understanding was all wrong. Really I didn't come here to love God like I thought, coming here wasn't even my decision. God brought me here, India has been God's gift to me. I now understand the reason I am in India is to learn how to let God love me.

Laura Thomas
Sisters of Charity of Nazareth Ministry Corps

Hymn

The students do not know why I am there,
nor do they care.
When I go to school, I must take only my love—
most of them do not get smiled at very often;
they usually see stern faces.

So they hug me and smile at me—
a woman they hardly know—
because I smile first.

I look them in the eyes,
I affirm them for the people they are,
and I love them even when they are misbehaving.

That, I think, is the most important thing I can do.

My grand hopes and expectations of volunteering
have been replaced by the desire
to be sure I smile at each of my students
every day.

That is why I now do what I do.

Sarah Friede
Marianist Voluntary Service Communities

Closing

Gracious God, you call us in mysterious ways, and sometimes we do not even understand the real call until later. Give us generous hearts, open minds, and strong wills to follow you, and may your peace be with us. Amen.

2

Letting Go of Easy Answers

God of surprises, help us let go of easy answers and pre-conceived notions. May we abandon ourselves to what is real, here and now. You are all truth, and your truth is found in what is real. Peel off my fingers that clutch to my ways, which are not necessarily *your* ways.

Faithful God:
It seems to me that *volunteering* is going to get better,
and then harder,
easier to be myself,
then more difficult to know who that person is.

Lots of questions run through my mind lately.
I am faced with issues of social justice both here and
    abroad;
a thousand questions fly in my face and out of my
    mouth.

I am too conservative, too afraid of change,
too satisfied with the status quo to face the tough
    questions.

I am confused and somewhat angry.
I wonder what really goes on behind the scenes
of government and law.

Why is our government supporting the government in
    El Salvador?
Why do some people live in military states
where there are bodies at the curbside?

Why are there countries where murder is accepted,
a personal grief, not a national outrage?
Why does it seem that no matter how many people
    struggle and die,
still nothing changes?

I have absolutely no answers, millions more questions.
I know so little, I understand nothing.

I feel a war raging in my head.
My beliefs are being challenged,
my old value system shaking.

Cara A. DeNuccio
Jesuit Volunteer Corps

Reading

As the seasons change from summer to fall, I find my focus changing. Fall is a time that urges me to be gentle with myself and others. This season invites me to focus not so much on where I need to go, but to ask for the grace to recognize the life already present around me. It's a time for letting go and trusting in the eventual abundance of spring.

I wouldn't dare make such a sweeping statement if I weren't backed up by the trees. Trees respect the natural rhythm of growth. In fall, they slowly drop their leaves, one by one, and go into a state that resembles death. So if I become frustrated at times with work or community, maybe I too need to allow the expectations that are weighing me down to drop. In order to bring greater fruit and life to people, I may need to slow down and rest first—to enter a season of fall.

I will be remembered for the way I lived, not for how much I did. The quality of my work and my effectiveness with people are at stake if I don't respond to the changing seasons in my life—the call to fall. Yes, I think I will join the trees and ask for the experience of being empty for a period of time. It's scary, but I hope that I may be filled. Because nature abhors a vacuum, I just might be pleasantly amazed by what fills my branches, usually something more joyful and incredible than anything I could have planned alone.

Patrik Davis
Jesuit Volunteer Corps

Hymn

"If we are to be pilgrims of peace and justice,
we must expect the desert."

These words of Dom Helder Camara remind me
of Jesus' forty days in the desert,
and of the three temptations he endured.

I wonder in what ways I have been tested
here in the desert that is my ministry.

I realize that through action, intention, or desire,
I have fallen to all three.

First Satan said,
"If you are the Son of God,
turn these stones into bread."
After months of trying, I realize
that not only can I not make stones into bread,
but I cannot make homeless people "domiciled,"
make alcoholics sober,
or make broken people whole.
Only God's grace in receptive hearts can do that.
But how I crave that power!

Then Satan said,
"If you are the Son of God, jump off this tower,
and the angels will save you."
I have no godly guarantee
that the poor won't break my heart,
or my spirit,
or my neck!
Yet how I yearn for that security.

Finally Satan proffered,
"I will give you all that you see,
if you will fall down and worship me."
Often I fall to the longings of my dark side:
longing for a well-dressed,
well-respected,
well-compensated place in the kingdom of this world.
And how I desire that glamour!

God, let me not forget the flowers in the desert!
I cannot turn stones to bread,
but with loving outreach I can turn a heart of stone
into two hands serving bread in our soup line.

I have no assurance of angelic protection,
but I can be assured that God will be revealed
in new and completely unexpected ways
in old and completely unexpected faces,
if only I open my eyes.

The lure of luxury may be strong,
but with a little grace I can resist
my lust for shrimp scampi and silk scarves

long enough to appreciate the beauty, honesty, and "unencumberedness" of simple living.

Given enough grace, I might even be able to appreciate lentils!

Christine M. Silsby
Freedom House

Closing

God, your ways are not our ways. And even though we know that your way leads to faith, hope, and love, we often resist walking your way. May we accept the grace you offer to get out of our ruts, to let go of our shaky security, and to walk with you in truth and light. Amen.

3

Adapting

Opening

God, you reveal yourself in many guises, and you draw us out of ourselves in many different ways. Teach us to be not wishy-washy but flexible, adaptable, ready to listen to our sisters and brothers, and ready to do your will.

Psalm

Merciful God:
Before, I lived by myself in a big house.
As a missionary, I live in a shelter with all God's people.

Before, I drove a sports car for a status symbol.
As a missionary, I drive the agency station wagon
    as a privilege.

Before, I wore expensive clothes
    and worried about my looks.
As a missionary, I wear simple outfits
    and never looked better.

Before, I bought whatever I wanted with credit cards.
As a missionary, I accept donations
    for the things I need.

Before, I asked for whatever I wanted God to do.
As a missionary, I give thanks for all God has done.

Before, I went to Sunday Mass and felt content.
As a missionary, I go to daily Mass
    and know it is not enough.

Before, I was an individual trying to do some good
    in my small town.
As a missionary, I am part of a larger community,
    the people of God.

Doreen M. Zeleny
Missionary Cenacle Volunteers

21

Reading

In the back of my head, a voice was saying, "I can't believe you're doing this." I aimed our big green jeep at a stream, drove downhill into the riverbed, and plunged into the water.

In central Venezuela during the dry season, the temperature reaches the nineties by midmorning, so I was already sweating before I reached the river. But intentionally driving into water of an unknown depth made me break into an even heavier sweat.

"Are you sure this is what we're supposed to be doing?" I asked my husband.

"Yes, yes, this is the right direction," Matt responded calmly.

Maybe it's because Matt is from Indiana—and not from the Motor City of Detroit—that he could remain so nonchalant about committing such an unnatural act with an automobile.

But there we were, neophyte missionaries, trying to get back to town from a far-flung Indian village. There weren't any paved roads out that way, and only a handful of the streams in our path had bridges. Even crossing the hand-fashioned log bridges was nerve-wracking enough for me.

Somehow, with fervent prayers, we made it through that river and easily emerged dry and unscathed. In fact, my husband and I forded many streams and rivers during our two years as Catholic pastoral agents in a large rural zone of central Venezuela. I eventually learned to calm down and get through the crossings without such panic.

I think my memory of the first river crossing is so vivid because it represented for me a crossing into the unknown. At that moment, I knew at a gut level—a survival level—that I had left behind the North American way of life and had entered another. To be able to adapt to and respect another culture would take many such "crossings" and an ability to laugh at myself in the process.

Carol Schuck Scheiber
Logos Translators

In the peace of our day, love flows between and among.
We live to learn, as we learn to give.
Our lives become simple and the complicated
    falls away.
And in sharing our lives, we bring peace to others.

I am perched atop the peak of my roof.
The sky is a faded blue-gray.
A cool breeze blows desperately
    over the ragged neighborhood,
where the buildings sag from lack of care,
much like their human inhabitants.

A clearing among the buildings is used as a parking lot,
garbage dump, and playground,
where the neighborhood kids learn from what they see.

A war is being waged here,
a violent war among souls
    who cling to destructive ways.
My mind reels to find the answer before the darkness.
But my hand grows weary and my light is gone. . . .

Hymn

A fan hummed, cars idled by,
planes flew overhead, radios played, a baby cried.

I listened for an emotion,
but a bird chirped, a wind gently rustled,
    someone whistled.

I listened for an emotion as the sounds melted
    and became one.
Occasionally, one sound stood out among the rest
    and then faded,
then another rose and faded.

In a short passage of time, I heard the neighborhood
swell in anger, then happiness,
fall from pain, and settle to mellow comfort.
In the same breath, I heard my neighborhood laugh
    and cry.

How long did it take for the rhythm
    to become apparent?
I don't know.
For each person the rhythm is different.

And for all, every minute is a beat of music
that will compose a year of song.
With each year, our songs become more intricate,
    alluring,
chronicling our lives until they become one,
    permanently.

We fragment and strike a path of our own
that will lead us to a common ground.
Our fear is that our paths will never cross again,
and our faith is knowing that they will.

As I lay on my bed and listened for an emotion,
I heard the ballad of a lifetime!
May we grow in strength and our love encompass all.

Laura Compton
Marianist Voluntary Service Communities

Closing

Faithful God, may we hear the changing rhythms in ourselves, in other people, and in your creation. May we
move with love to the new tempos, surprising invita-
tions, and unexpected needs. Amen.

4

Learning Acceptance

Holy Friend, teach us the virtue of acceptance, which means "to receive willingly." You give us grace to give. Now we ask for grace to learn acceptance.

Opening

Patient God:
I have always struggled with the concept of acceptance.
The very word immediately sends a rush of negatives
that point an insistent finger at me.
Things that we are challenged to accept
are things that we usually don't like.

Psalm

To agree *to* does not mean to agree *with*.
When we are called to accept ideas, people,
    or situations,
we are asked to live in reality—
a reality that includes the whole picture
and not just our view, our belief, our way.

Acceptance calls us to look at other lives,
other modes of living and being.
I may receive you willingly,
though your ways seem different to me.
And I may agree *to* understand your way,
though I may not agree *with* it.

Acceptance begins with me.
To be Christlike, we must accept first,
and then be open to work with what we have accepted.
I am still learning, and I thank God for the challenge
to really see things as God does—as God accepts.

Dagmar Arango
Marianist Voluntary Service Communities

Reading

There's a cunning lawyer in the Gospel of Luke. When told by Jesus that he should love his neighbor as himself, he did what any good lawyer would do—he looked for a loophole. He asked, "And who is my neighbor?"

Who is my neighbor?

I used to mull over this question a lot when I first came to High Springs. Then, I was a stranger in a strange town—a guy who asked for change to the pop machine and was gently corrected, "You want pop? Son, we don't sell pop. Those there are cold drinks."

I decided that the best way to answer the neighbor question was to visit a few churches. After all, isn't that where people go to be neighborly?

A church on the northwest side of town caught my eye. I was hesitant. I had never worshiped in a black church, nor had I known many black people in my life. They had never lived in my neighborhood.

But I felt driven. Who is my neighbor? Something about that question, something about myself, compelled me to visit there one Sunday.

My determination, however, evaporated as I approached the church. I paused at the front door. Would they welcome me? What would they think? Me, a single, white man coming alone to a black church. Could they overlook my Yankee accent and chronic sunburn?

I called up enough courage to open the door and peek around the corner. Everyone in the church fell silent. For me, it was as if time stood still. The pastor, who had gathered them all into the back pews for a meeting, looked up and asked, "Can I help you?" Obviously he was thinking, "This poor white boy looks lost."

I stuttered and stammered. Basically, I panicked. I waved my hands and said, "I just came here to worship, but I can go now. I don't mean to bother you. I'll just leave out this door, right here."

"No, no, join us," he replied. "We're having a meeting now, but come back in about ten minutes."

I paced outside. After a few minutes I thought, "This is ridiculous." But just as I turned and headed for my car, a young-looking man came out of the church, grabbed my hand and said with a broad smile, "Welcome, brother, it's great to have ya!"

He led me back in. I was introduced to most everyone there and shown to a front pew. As I sat, stunned by their warmth and friendliness, someone hauled out a big bass drum. A few tambourines were passed around. As last minute stragglers took their seats, a woman behind me started humming an old spiritual. Then suddenly, the whole congregation exploded into gospel music mayhem.

For an hour and a half, the music stirred my soul. I swayed and clapped as much as my ingrained Swedish-Lutheran sensibilities would allow (which isn't much). And I prayed in silence, while others thanked God aloud for the blessings God had given.

When worship had ended, I was invited to my first taste of "Southern cookin'," a fellowship dinner of fried chicken, gumbo, and corn bread. It was delicious! It was also a chance to talk with and get to know these new neighbors of mine.

Who is my neighbor?

When that question comes to mind, I look back at that Sunday. Although I belong to another church, I return occasionally to this special group of people, these friends who helped me overcome the chains of my own fear and prejudice.

I return because when they ask themselves, "Who is my neighbor?" they look in my direction, beyond our differences, take my hand and say, "Welcome, brother, it's great to have ya!"

Greg Darr
Catholic Volunteers in Florida

Hymn

Jesus, passing through Jericho,
spotted a little man named Zacchaeus up in a tree.
Smiling at Zacchaeus, Jesus said,
"Come down, my friend,
I need a place to sleep tonight,
and I have chosen your house."
Happily, Zacchaeus took his guest home.

But the critics grumbled,
"This guy's a tax collector, a sinner too."

Zacchaeus pulled himself up to his full, but short,
    height and said,
"Master, look, I'll give half of everything I own
    to the poor,
and make it right with anyone who thinks
    I cheated them."

Amused, Jesus told him,
"You have found salvation, son of Abraham and Sarah.
I have come to find and save those who are lost."

(Luke 19:1–10)

Closing

Forgiving God, Jesus loved an open and accepting spirit.
You accept us just as we are. Teach us to accept other
people for who they are. May we learn from one another
and love one another. Amen.

5

God's Providence

Trustworthy God, we don't always trust you. Forgive our doubts about your provident care. May we let go of our need to control so that we can see, understand, and accept your constant, faithful love.

Opening

We put a lot of trust in the Holy Spirit
because, God knows, we were blundering a lot.
But then we figured,
what did Moses know before he got started?
What did Jeremiah know?

Psalm

Having carried a child in rural Venezuela—
where there were a few more risks than here—
made me more dependent on God.

At a certain point, things are out of your control.
Even if there had been a high-tech birthing center
    a block away,
who's really in control of what happens?

It's not me who's bringing life;
it's not Matt; it's not the doctor.
It's God who's in control.
That's a very Latin American way to look at it.

During a terrible drought,
    with livestock dying every day,
one man said, "Don't worry.
God knows we need rain; our rain will come."

Living with people who have a fundamental reliance
    on God
was a factor in deciding to have our child
    in that faraway land;
trying to continue that reliance might be harder here.

Carol Schuck Scheiber
Logos Translators

Reading

"Blessed are the poor in spirit; the kingdom of heaven is theirs."

(Matt. 5:3)

"Ask and the gift shall come; seek and you shall find. . . . Whatever you ask of God will be given to you."

(Matt. 7:7)

The rolling, green hills surrounded me and the red clay ribbon of road cut a straight line ahead of me and my little red motorcycle. It was a beautiful day in the Bolivian Amazon basin in the Acre valley, and I was on my way to a village some thirty kilometers from our home. About ten kilometers outside of Cobija, the town where I lived, I remembered the old Indian couple Doña María and Don José. Over a month had passed since my last visit, and with plenty of time before my next appointment, I thought I would stop by.

I hid the motorcycle in the bushes and started down the narrow path to the home of the old couple. I enjoyed the peacefulness of the thirty-minute walk. At times, the graceful trees formed an arc over my head like a green cathedral. I could hear the chattering monkeys, but I couldn't see them. The sounds of the birds and insects filled me with wonder and joy. The humid fragrance of the rain forest hung in the air.

When I was about halfway to their home, I met José. His full head of white hair was in disarray as usual, his patched shirt wrinkled but clean. His broad, bare feet were strong on the jungle floor, as rooted in it as the trees that surrounded us. "Where are you going?" I asked. "Oh, Marianita," he said, "I have come to meet you." "Meet me?" "Yes, María sent me to meet you. She told me that you were coming to see her today. I'm very worried about her. She has been in bed about a week and cannot eat anything."

Together José and I arrived at their home, two buildings in a small clearing. Both structures had thatched roofs; neither had walls. The larger shelter had a bed on one side standing on the pounded and well-swept dirt floor. Mosquito netting was draped over it, and I knew that María was resting inside. The other building was the kitchen lean-to. Tea and soup were brewing on the open-pit fire. José headed off to the kitchen. As I moved the mosquito netting aside, María smiled up at me. Her small, wrinkled face was full of happiness. Her hair was combed, and a long gray braid draped over her shoulder. Her neck was adorned with red, black, and white strands of beads that she had made from the seeds of the forest she loved so well.

"I knew that you would come," she said. "I've been praying for your visit, and God told me that you would come this afternoon."

Marianne Dunne
Maryknoll Associate Lay Missioner Program

Hymn

Long hours have preceded him
in journeying steps across the mission
roads to his oblivion. Long hours of
steps that lead him through his daily
tasks—and leave behind the footprints

shoeless in the sands. His head in
silence and in age is bent—to catch
the glimpse of words in gentle tones of
voice, who is his only friend. And
David marks his pace with crooked,
crippled evenness. No urgencies to
stir him on. No anxieties for earthly things.
Or ears to hear the scoffing and the jests
of younger boys—who harry him. His
mind is bent to godly things. And
in his rags, long before the day begins, he makes
his long and torturing trek to Mass and
there greets his Master. Though he in sickness
and ill health is bent, he is not exempt from
kneeling profoundly. In penitence.
And making his thanks.
For daily food. And for a roof. And for the
other simple needs and joys that shape his life.
His almost sightless gaze takes him once again
into the white-hot African sun, and down that long
and lonely path that leads to his obscurity—
and sees into his past. And, smilingly, he passes by—
crooked hand on crooked stick to guide him on. And
never once this selfsame hand is seen
outstretched for alms or seeking other goods.
On charity alone he lives—and asks for
not one thing more
than has been given him!

Emily Kulchsyki
Los Angeles Lay Mission Helpers

Closing

Brother Jesus, thank you for a comforting word. Keep
close to me. I don't ask to see the distant future; one step
at a time is enough for me. But one thing I do ask. Let me
feel your hand, let me hear your gentle voice, and lead
me on. Amen.

David Suley
Los Angeles Lay Mission Helpers

6

God's Presence

Let us remember that we always stand on holy ground, because our God permeates all of life. Praise to you, ever-present, loving God.

Opening

Today, Agnes made me feel bad
because I didn't know what "First Friday" was or means.
My prayer isn't dictated from some religious doctrine
or some prayer book
nor is my relationship with God.

Psalm

My love for God is alive and now and dynamic
        and every day.
My prayer is my attitude, my interactions with others,
my time alone, my bicycle ride to work,
        my abstinence from meat,
my desire to dance in church or at Pe-Te's.

First Friday, love God my way.
You will see that you have your way
        that God has given you.
Full of joy, full of living, love God your way.
Look inside and trust your spirit and laugh and cry
        and sing.

First Friday, same as any day
Each moment, a brand new moment,
        that only God can bring.
First Friday or is this Tuesday?
All my days are gifts from God.

First Friday, just like any day
I want to allow myself to be used by love.
Love is God, just like every day,
and God is all I want.

First Friday and every other day
my life and love I give to you.

Laura Thomas
Sisters of Charity of Nazareth Ministry Corps

Reading

I'm realizing that God loves me. The work has been good and important for me. But it has been the people I have met that have been India for me. From the welcome song and dance in Mokama to all of the sisters here. And how could I forget my favorite fruit vendors in the Golmuri market and the jewelry lady who wants me to take her home. And the babies at the children's home with all of their wet and dirty diapers and their wonderful smiles. And the older children and girls at the home, and the lady who cooks for us in the convent, all of whom have been my private Hindi teachers. Dancing the hokey-pokey with the children at Gyan Deep School, followed by the bunny hop. Being invited into some family's home in Mosabani and being the recipient of such warm Indian hospitality. And maybe my favorite people of all, the drivers of the three-wheeled taxis or auto rickshaws, who all seem to have something very strange about them. In November, on my first train journey alone, I traveled to Mokama and the stars were shining so bright. When I got off the train at 4:30 in the morning, I wanted to sing and dance in the crisp morning air under the beautiful starry skies. God was telling me again that he loves me and reminding me that all of the beautiful people I was meeting in India were all his gift to me.

Laura Thomas

The crickets are chirping as the night softly descends.
The day has been filled
with the now-familiar echoes of rain on the tin roof.

Soon the galaxy of stars begins to sparkle
through the clean, cool, night air.
The sweet smell of damp earth
joins the crickets and stars in a celebration of life.
A celebration of life—after a year in Malawi,
I think this sums up my feelings.
Celebrating life—
rising in the early hours as the sun only begins its daily
     journey,
joining together to celebrate God's blessings.

It isn't difficult to feel a bit closer to God here—
the green mountains—
the towering trees filling the air
with the sound of the wind passing,
bringing life-giving rain or soul-warming sunshine—
the white clouds—the colorful flowers—
     the lovely birds.

There is harmony of life among the people here, too—
a smile—a warm handshake—a rose—a cup of tea—
little ways of saying they care.
The little things build the foundations of our lives—
of our love—a harmony of purpose—a joy!

Coletta Furin Maksimik
Lay Mission Helpers Association

Hymn

God present, thank you for all the signs of your dwelling with us. Open our sight, hearing, taste, and touch that we may sense your presence here and now. Praise and thanks to you, always-with-us God. Amen.

Closing

7

Touched by the Poor

Your poor people touch our heart, creator God. May we detect your voice in their voices, and may we learn their wisdom.

Psalm

My life is becoming more and more
    intimately intertwined
with those of my Chilean friends
    and North American housemates:

Sharing the birth and baptism
    of Vicente and Raquel's son,
Sharing Teresa's pain over the unjust detention of her son,
Dancing at our costume party with friends here
    in the *población*.

Spending the day with Lily:
singing, hiking in the foothills,
    washing clothes and sewing,
Praying for a friend who has been forced into hiding,
Helping Humberto with his exercises
to regain muscle strength and coordination.

Accompanying those who are ill,
and gratefully receiving visitors when I was ill.
Sharing, crying, and laughing
with Chilean peers during our recent retreat.

People like Angelica and Sara
are touching me profoundly with their lives—
their simplicity, questioning, and service to others
amid the illness, poverty, and at times
desperate situations of their own lives.

I am learning a deeper sense of humility.
Be assured, however, that I am happy here—
thankful for the gift of life and the opportunity
    to be living the struggles and challenges
with the people in La Faena.

Anne Attea
Holy Cross Associates Volunteer Program

Silence. Presence. Family. Giving. Strength. Deep Faith. Respect. Alcohol. Brokenness. Spirit. . . . All are words that remind me of the Oglala, the Lakota.

Never before have I experienced such power in a land or a people, such quiet strength. I remember women with men's hands and deep lines in their faces; women who have raised three generations of children; men and women who have trusted deeply through much pain and suffering; families that have struggled through alcoholism; songs that stir the very depths of one's being. These are people who are always ready to give, even when they have nothing. I must admit that now, after being away from the reservation for several months, I realize how stingy my "generosity" is. To the Lakota, giving is a part of life. If one is in need, someone else meets the need. I remember a woodpile appearing in the yard of a woman who couldn't get her own wood. There are no homeless children on the reservation because someone, relative or not, gives them a permanent home.

The Lakota love to feast, and in doing so, they always prepare too much food, so that *wateca* (pronounced wa-ta-cha) buckets for leftovers are taken home by all the guests.

After a death, a year is spent preparing gifts for people who touched that person's life. Above all, time is given. The Lakota do not understand our need to rush and to do. To them it is more important to spend hours just being with one another. The gift of time is a sign of respect to be shared with others.

I remember going to the home of a traditional Lakota family. Their home consisted of a couple of rough rooms. The living room served as a bedroom. We went to share a rosary, for although Grandmother had died a month or two before, the family still carried on her tradition. After the rosary, we were asked to share part of their feast, which had been prepared for a baptism that afternoon. We ate. As traditional respect dictates, they ate later—after the baptism—yet they had shared with us.

The gifts I have received from the Lakota are countless. They offer what they have, which is what they are—nothing more, nothing less!

Cyle Neilson
Marianist Voluntary Service Communities

Hymn

My lay missionary experience has been like sand.

Sand can be too hot to walk on.
   You take it a few steps at a time—
      then you throw down your towel and
      cool the bottoms of your feet.
      Take refuge. Begin again.

Sand can sting your legs.
   As the wind blows it, it cuts across
      the top of the land
      and blasts its way into you—ouch.

It's intruding—imagine the tiniest speck in your eye.
   You can think of nothing else
      while it's in there.

Ahhh. But sand can feel so good.
   It molds itself to the contours of your body.
      It massages your feet as you walk along.

You get bogged down in it.
   Sand forces you to slow down.
      You cannot move quickly through sand.

It can warm you to lie back on it.
   It can cool you.
      It takes its cue from the sun.

And you know that sand—it gets into every
   crevice of your body.
      Sand finds its way—it works its way in,

Into the bends in your ear, the tiniest grit
   right at your temple,
      up at your hairline above your forehead.
         It falls down as you rub gently, beckoning it.

It stays with you—you can't get rid of it,
   it keeps turning up—even just the tiniest bit.

In the bottom of the bathtub you thought you
   had rinsed clean.
In the lining of that bag
   shifting from
      corner to corner.

Jeannie Ritter
Oblates of Mary Immaculate Lay Missionary in Zambia

God of the poor, "Individuals are making an impact on my life with their faith and perseverance, despite their continual difficulties and crises. My life is changing—not severely or rapidly, but it is changing. I am more aware, more sensitized to the many different needs of people in my life and of other people in your world. I have no idea where this road will take me, but it's a good road to be on. Thanks for my friends who accompany me on the journey." Amen.

Anne Attea

Closing

8

God's Poor

Opening

Poor and needy people surround us, and we still find it easy to look right through them. Light of Lights, open our eyes to see your poor. Suffering Servant, open our hands to serve them.

Psalm

I have witnessed that poverty is not a rare commodity owned by those with few possessions.

Each person who needs companionship,
love, or concern is poor.

In laying my hands upon my patients in treatment,
I have felt the healing of God's spirit manifested.

In opening my eyes to each person,
I have seen deep scars and overwhelming joys.

In opening my ears,
I have known contagious laughter and haunting sorrow.

Angie Evans
Marianist Voluntary Service Communities

Reading

As Jerry gets up off his sleeping mat shaking (with delirium tremens) on Christmas night at the drop-in center, he says, "I have to stop drinking this liquid garbage, it's killing me!" A few short months ago in the hospital, the doctors gave Jerry only six months to live if he didn't quit drinking. After leaving the hospital, Jerry came to visit me, raised his right hand, and swore to God that he would never drink again. His departing statement still rings in my head, "I want to live." Jerry's intentions were good. The reality is that Jerry has been a homeless alcoholic for the past twelve years.

Two days later, I found Jerry drunk, lying facedown on the sidewalk on Thirteenth Street. As I stood over him, I wondered: "What causes one to drink himself to death?

And when Jerry does die—who will care? Who will notice that he is gone?"

    Well, three days ago, it happened. Jerry was found dead in a friend's apartment. He was afforded the dignity of dying inside a friend's home, instead of on the street alone. He died of a brain hemorrhage.

Richard Steineman
Marianist Voluntary Service Communities

Hymn

6:30 p.m. and in they come,
one by one or in groups.
Dinner is close to being served.

Many have had a very long day on the streets—
walking around aimlessly,
	without meaning or direction,
or drinking in quiet corners and
trying to stay warm in libraries
	and fast-food restaurants.

They look forward to their meal of the day.
Some share their experiences.
Many talk endlessly, even if no one listens.

After dinner the TV is turned on.
Others randomly take showers—
clean clothes are distributed.
The TV goes off at 11 p.m.
All head off to their place of rest.

Midnight. About three dozen people are snoring.
Fifty mattresses are laid out in neat rows
	across the union hall floor.

Another sixty-five people in an adjacent room—
some sleeping on concrete, others in chairs,
and still others avoiding sleep altogether.

This is a home where you sleep with strangers,
and everyone sleeps with their clothes on.
The sleeping here can be difficult at times—
continuous coughing, hacking,
and an occasional scream from a nightmare,
or the clang of a smuggled wine bottle hitting the floor.

Last night, I spotted a man drinking his shaving lotion.
He said he needed something for his nerves.
These are the Cincinnati street people.

Richard Steineman

Closing

Holy Friend, may we be your hands of healing and voice
of comfort. But also give us courage to act for justice.
Amen.

9

Simplicity

Opening

Loving God, help us to focus on one thing: doing your will, which ultimately means loving our neighbors as we love ourselves. Only this will bring about justice and peace. May we simplify our lives, so that we are able to cling more firmly to what is eternal and essential.

Psalm

My heart cannot accept a society
that exists to obtain worldly goods
over that which inherently
pleases the human soul.

The price for spiritual fulfillment
and for love
is worth all that people find
a need for through substance.

There is immeasurable joy to be found
in a child's embrace
in a warm kiss
in a friend's smile.

Rita Abdallah
Jesuit Volunteer Corps

Reading

We felt a little bit silly. My husband and I—Catholic lay missionaries just starting out in Venezuela—were sleeping in a room with an air conditioner grinding loudly. Meanwhile, a Panare Indian and his son slept just a few feet away in a hammock outdoors. They had passed by our temporary home where we were studying Spanish and asked to stay the night because they were far from their village.

We mused at how odd we must seem to them to be using a loud machine to cool down the cement room that had heated up to 115 degrees that day. The obvious solution to combating the indoor heat was to stay out of it; sleep outside in the cooler night air.

43

We've since left our hot cement house with its air conditioner. Now we live in a town that has electricity for just six hours in the evening. When it's too hot to sleep indoors, we simply string up our hammocks outdoors, Venezuelan style.

Venezuelans with their simpler style have taught me a lot about living with less and how it can be a good thing, even if their simple lifestyle includes some serious injustices in education and health care. One cannot romanticize their rudimentary lives as pure pastoral bliss.

Still, for all that they lack, they have something I don't have. In their uncluttered lives, campesinos have a dependence on God that I rarely encounter in my technological, self-sufficient society. "God will surely send us the rains. I'm sure of it. He knows all our needs," commented one young man during a drought. When cattle or members of a family get sick, when a widow is left penniless, or when other calamities strike, God and the saints are the first ones to whom the Venezuelans turn. Their simplicity of lifestyle does encourage two good qualities: an openness to God and a life that revolves around family, friends, and nature.

Carol Schuck Scheiber
Logos Translators

Hymn

Jesus tells us that we are blessed, happy,
    if we can live this poverty.
This is the poverty and simplicity I wish to live.

Overwhelmed by the intensity and breadth
of the poverty in which I was submerged,
and by my inability to relate to those in need,
I cried out,
"What the hell do you want from me, Lord?"
My crying out was all I had.

My "simple lifestyle" would always be safe and secure.
I had family and friends I could count on.
The clients I worked with had no one.
I questioned my poverty more and more.

And then I recalled
Rahner saying something about love
as falling into the incomprehensibility
    of the mystery of God.

In my weakness and desperation,
impoverished and emptied of all other possibilities,
I fell to my knees and into God's love.
And on my knees, I understood.

I began to discover that true poverty of spirit and soul
must not be limited to material fact or even spiritual
    aspiration.
To be "poor in spirit" is to come before God
empty, in absolute need, and to cry out.
My cry was not only true prayer but poverty of spirit.

Love is a posture of poverty before God,
love that risks caring.
To *care* means "to cry out"
as well as "to have concern for."
When we truly love, we care,
and thus we cry out in our pain and hurt
    and emptiness.
Immersed in that love,
    we learn what it is to be poor in spirit.

As I grew in poverty, I learned
how to love more passionately,
compassionately, and intimately.

Let us cry out together,
learn from one another how to grow poor.
Let us place ourselves in proper posture before God,
and together grow in intimate friendship
    with Jesus Christ,
who came to proclaim the Good News to the poor.
Let us together live simply
and build the Reign of Christ here among us.

Tony Nicotera
Jesuit Volunteer Corps

Good Shepherd, you came to lead us to peace, light, and
life. Teach us purity of heart to will only the coming of
your Reign. May we simplify our lives so that we keep
your will before our eyes: to love our neighbors as ourselves. Please teach us simplicity. Amen.

Closing

10

Compassion

Always gracious God, teach us your compassion. May we learn from Jesus, who healed lepers, raised the dead, and fed his hungry followers. Compassion. O God, teach us compassion.

4:26 p.m. Somewhere between Lucknow and Gaya—
We both have good eyes and ears.
We both have good hands and our noses.
And we both have good hearts
    which are keeping us alive.

I can tell this because we are both moving.
And I can see your heart by the emotions in your eyes.
But you have no legs
And I have no compassion.

As you hobble by with your tin extended,
    I give my offering
Afraid to look in your eyes.
There are so many eyes to look into here in this country.
And I watch the natives as they look away,
And I assume this is how I should also behave.

But I can't and I don't want to.
You are a child of God as am I
And you are my brother
    just as much as the people I have known all my life.

I don't want to give you money, but love.
Which will serve you better,
    and whose needs am I trying to meet?
It is love that is of value.

Your brother and my brother walks by.
He has good legs, but he is blind.
He walks by with his hand extended
And no one acknowledges his existence.
What kind of life is that?

He walks by the religious, and they don't even look
to see if he is a man or a woman,
blind or crippled, young or old.

Why can't I love everyone? I don't understand it.

Laura Thomas
Sisters of Charity of Nazareth Ministry Corps

Reading

Early Easter morning, I was visiting in Chichicastenango, Guatemala. Wrapped in my new Indian blanket, I went out into the cold mountain dawn. The town square was filling with shelters from which the Mayas would later sell food, jewelry, clothing, masks, and so on. The smoke of copal incense suffused the air around the front door of the church. I went in and sat down in the back. Not understanding the language, I prayed my own prayers.

Suddenly a little boy, probably Quiché Maya, appeared in front of me, talking. I caught the word *dinero*. I knew that he wanted money, and I held out my empty hands. Then on impulse, I opened my blanket and asked, "Are you cold?"

"*Sí, frío,*" he answered, and sat down by me, snuggling close. I wrapped my arm and the blanket around him. We sat very still for about fifteen minutes, watching the service.

Several people walked by and stared at us as if wondering how the North American white woman and the small Quiché Mayan had gotten together. I wondered too. It seemed like the coming together of opposites— white and Indian, female and male, old and young, rich and poor. Yet in our common humanity, we were so alike and both children of one God.

After a while his body and my soul warmed, and he jabbered something and left with an "adios." (I smiled at that word, familiar from listening to "The Lone Ranger" in my childhood.) Shortly after, I left too, peaceful and content. I felt as if I had received the Easter message of compassion and reconciliation directly.

Barbara Jo Dickens
Catholic Volunteers of Florida

Hymn

5:10 p.m.
I don't know if they are everywhere,
but there are many who are poor,
    many who are begging.
I think of home and the homeless there
and the people who ask for money there.

I used to not give anything,
and I would quickly walk by.
I didn't want to give them money
for something I viewed as self-destructive,
aren't all the homeless alcoholics or drug addicts?
Finally I decided
who am I to judge
what the person uses the money for?

5:25 p.m.
I began to talk to the people
and ask them what they needed.
I would treat them with the same respect
that I would give to anyone.
We have to understand
that no one life
is more important than another.

An angel walks by and sings his song.
He is blind but continues to praise his god.
He gives me his love with his song and his voice.

Laura Thomas

Closing

Sometimes you teach us compassion in wonderful, surprising ways. May we grow in our compassion for all of your people, loving, compassionate God. Open our souls and hands. Amen.

11

Children

Opening

Parent to Us All, your children suffer, especially because they have no power. All too often they become victims of violence, greed, and avaricious exploitation. Teach us to "let the little children come" to us (Matt. 19:14).

Psalm

I took a chance.
I told Dexter that I care about him.
He told me that I would be just like the rest of them—

As soon as he screwed up,
I would turn my back
and act like I didn't even know him.

I've realized that he has touched my heart,
but does he know it?
So maybe I'll never see
how much I've meant to him,
but I'd like to think that somehow,
someway, I made a difference.

Dagmar Arango
Marianist Voluntary Service Communities

Reading

During free time in class that day, Mercedes came to see me. All I can see in my mind's eye is her beautiful little face, the large, almond-shaped eyes fringed with dark lashes, and the curve of her cheeks.

"Can you give me that prayer?" she asked me as her eyes became sparkling pools of liquid. She sought the prayer for families I had quickly scribbled down in preparation for class—sacred and mystical to her—her courageous grasp for some goodness, for some good fortune in her young life.

"Is there something happening with your family right now?"

"No."

"But sometimes?"

"Yes," she replied, but would not share more.

49

I wanted to convey my understanding and warmth to her with a touch, because I could not find the words. I wrote down the prayer for her.

Just recently, I received a letter and some drawings from Mercedes. Again she requested the prayer for families. I made one up, because I did not remember how I had phrased the original. How I wish Mercedes knew that the longing in her heart is the sweetest and most powerful prayer of all, and Jesus holds it tenderly.

What better way to understand this mystery than in the words of the Author of the Universe: "Let the little children come unto me. . . . I will wipe every tear from their eyes."

Stephanie J. Cortes
Mission of Friendship

Hymn

nobody's child

yesterday
i spent some time with you
dreaming sunrises
playing in clouds
hiding tomorrow's tears

you are nobody's child
lost
alone in crowded streets
finding a place to be

all that you have is in a plastic bag
strength
livelihood
memories
you carry them with you
like rocks
your only possessions

yet you'd give it all
if i'd take it
but it is nothing to me

i've heard them say
if you look north
you will never see
a sunrise

perhaps if i'd stayed longer
you could have taught me
to glimpse sunrises

to see beyond the dirt
to feel the sadness
of your soul

if only i had a pebble
of your courage
i would not have left you
to walk
alone

where will you be
when I have the courage
to find you
again

Georgine Vickerd
Scalabrinian Missionaries in Mexico

God, protector of children, hear our prayer: "Sometimes I wonder, how can our relationship last? We have nothing in common. Your body is broken, mine is whole. My spirit is broken, yours is whole. I need financial security, with you I am secure only in God's grace. I need words to comfort me, and you cannot speak. But when I look into your face, I can see all the answers in your trust, your fidelity, your patience, your sensitivity, your love, and the beauty of your being. I see a mirror of what you see in me, both of us truly children of God. I see that our love will endure forever, and I am peaceful. Thank you." Amen.

Closing

Mary Ann Walker
L'Arche Community, Rome

12

Teens at Risk

Opening

Understanding God, bless teenagers. For many of them this is a tough age. For those of us working with them, it's not such an easy time either. Guide us. Help us. And bless them.

Psalm

Hanging on our doorstep,
Dragging from his cigarette,
Standing strong and being tough,
On the inside he cries for help.
What can we do
to keep him in the grasp of our hearts?
The pull of his high is too strong.

Lynn Martin
Covenant House

Reading

The kids asked me why I was working at Saint John's if I had a degree from Harvard. Then when I told them that I would be leaving to start a new job, they were disappointed and upset. But I've decided to continue working at Saint John's as a volunteer on Sunday evenings after I begin my new job. These boys have become my friends. And I don't want to become just another "here one day, gone the next" friend. I want to help and to believe in these boys, precisely because they do have a future. With my investment banking background, I look at this year as an investment, and I want to see it flourish.

When I made the commitment to Saint John's for a year, I didn't realize how tough it would be to leave. Part of me will always be at Saint John's, and these young men I've laughed with, yelled at, disciplined, respected, and disrespected will always be a special part of me. Not that I am not looking forward to starting my new job; in fact, I'm psyched! I just didn't realize how much I enjoyed my work at Saint John's, until I actually started talking about it during my job interview.

One particular evening clarified my feelings for the boys. I accompanied eight boys to Madison Square Garden for a Knicks game and gave them some money for refreshments. We went to a deli nearby. I stood near the counter as they bought candy, chips, and soda. Two of the boys completed their purchases and were on their way out when they decided to buy a few more items. They attempted to come back in, but the store owner told them to beat it. I asked the owner if he had a problem with our kids. He snapped back, "Yeah. I do. I don't trust them in my store." This despite video cameras and four clerks watching like hawks. Just because the boys were black, the owner was automatically suspicious. Would he have had as many doubts if the kids had been white? I don't think so.

We were handing this guy about thirty dollars in business, and all he could think about was that our kids were criminals. Granted, some of our boys are not angels, but his lack of respect for them made me realize how much I really care for them. By insulting them, he insulted me. So, I'll be back with the boys on Sunday nights at Saint John's.

Paul Garavente
Marianist Voluntary Service Communities

Hymn

He looks hard,
He acts tough,
He doesn't fear.
He's bold and brazen,
He's violent.
Who is he?

He has had no stability;
People enter and exit his life.
Rejection hits; there is no love,
but there is an emptiness.
Drugs, alcohol, and crime
beat against him like waves
crashing against rocks.

He struggles to keep his head above water.
How does he deal with it?
Where does he turn?
He's gotta protect his image.
He can't let anyone know he needs help.
That's not cool.

How does one help him?
Listen . . . Listen . . . Listen
with patience and understanding.
Look through a magnifying glass,
then you will see:
his wanting attention
and starving for affection.
Searching for a way to take the lid off the jar.
To let out a simple cry;
but it's not simple—
the lid has been tight for too many years.

Fear is present;
Fear of rejection.
Lack of confidence exists.
He wants to open up,
but it seems too hard.
He wants to love,
but doesn't know how.

Who is he?
He's a teen.
Look through a magnifying glass
and then you will see.

Linda Dooley
Marianist Voluntary Service Communities

Closing

Wise God, give us wisdom, courage, and love to deal with young people at risk. The work is tough, but you call us to be with people who are most in need. Gracious God, be with us and with teens. Amen.

13

Battered Women

God, you hear the cries of poor people. Please hear the cries of women battered, abused, raped, and scorned. May your justice heal their wounds; may your peace empower them. May we be the agents of your healing and empowerment.

My mind
and my soul
have made a pact:

If there is a god,
      (her husband has been raping her two children
          for six years now.
      how could i have been so blind, she cries,
      as she hears her children's sobs torch shame and
      rage inside her)

and if there is a heaven,
      (her left eye pulses red;
      salt water oozes from under a swollen lid.
      the shoe in his hand never stomped the pavement
      as hard as her face)

and if heaven is a place,
      (her room was no more her own than her body:
      her father came into both and has not left her
          nightmares)

and if one day i should arrive there,
      (her husband locked her in one room
          for a year and a half.
      now she looks for a window to see herself)

and face God,
      (her boyfriend threw lye on her face.
      purple scar tissue merges
      with tissue on her scalp where he tried
          to "finish the job"
      with a knife)

and if God really is HE, the FATHER
then i am going to turn around and walk out.
Tara Murphy
Marianist Voluntary Service Communities

Reading

One of the hardest things for me in working at a shelter for battered women has been feeling out the boundary between accepting that a woman is responsible for her own decisions and attempting to facilitate a decision toward a life that gets out of the cycle of abuse.

In one instance, as a staff member, I had to tell a woman with a four-year-old child that she could no longer stay at the shelter. She had returned late and had been drinking, which violated two shelter policies. Upon leaving, her decision was to go back to her abuser, and her son left with her. As they were leaving, he said, "I don't want to go back and see my dad hit my mom with a belt." His brown eyes showed his pain. I felt responsible for making her circumstances more difficult, but realized that she is the only one who can leave the abuser, no matter how badly I want it for her and her child.

And as much as I want it for her, I have to remember that the questions to ask are not: "Why don't these women leave?" or "Why do these women go back?" The questions to ask are: "How do they leave?" or "How can they make it?" when life is so hard for them when they do leave. As one woman put it, the hardest part isn't being beaten, it's recovering.

Tara Murphy

Hymn

i whisper to the wind

i whisper to the wind, "he beats me."
i say a prayer at night that he will go.
i dare not speak the truth to others
my family, friends, and children: they all know.

they all whisper to the wind, "he beats her."
they say a prayer at night that he will go.
they dare not speak the truth to others
their family, friends, and children: they all know.

we've created a conspiracy of silence:
no one tells the other what she knows.
we all whisper to the wind, "he beats her,"
and say a prayer at night that he will go.

Voice of a battered woman
(from Lynora Campagna)
Marianist Voluntary Service Communities

Faithful God, "keeping the faith for me is believing that you go beyond the scope of the sexes and will provide relief for women who suffer from sexism, especially in the most extreme forms of rape and battering. It has been difficult to witness so much suffering through my work at the shelter for battered women and their children and not be changed by it." May our hearts change, and may our actions be turned to justice. God, give us courage. Amen.

Tara Murphy

Closing

14

AIDS

Opening

Holy Friend, we raise our hearts and minds to you. In the midst of suffering caused by HIV and AIDS, teach all of us compassion, love, courage, wisdom, and understanding.

Psalm

Creator,
God of the Synagogue, the Church,
the Temple, the Lodge, the Clearing;
God in and involved with the world in which we live;

God of those of us living at risk,
    and of those of us who are not;
God of Women, of Men, of Children;
Yahweh; Christ; Prophet; Father; Mother;
God of all Humankind, and of all Creation;

In whatever way we as separate human beings
    understand you,
be with us now in that understanding,
and in this, the present moment.

On this day, we focus our minds and our souls
    upon you,
we celebrate the prophets' teachings of peace,
    acceptance, diversity,
and we ache for the day
when these teachings will be embraced by all.

Today we also focus our hearts, God,
    in remembrance of those
known and unknown, loved and unloved,
who have died of complications due to AIDS.

Hear us, oh God, as we remember their names. . . .
[Pause to remember people who have died from AIDS.]

Will Smith
Marianist Voluntary Service Communities

Christ came into this world to show us that God cares for us in our present life and in the choices that we make each day, and not just to remind us of heaven. Christ came to participate in our daily lives—in our bliss and in our suffering, as we live them. He experienced human emotion in all its complexities. He laughed, and he cried.

Therefore, we remember not only those who have died but also those who are living with HIV or AIDS as well, right now, today, this very moment. We pray, God, that you hear us once again as we remember their names. . . . [Pause to remember people who are living with HIV or AIDS.]

Will Smith

We remember those who care;
> those who work for the agency, the hospital, and
> the hospice dedicated to people who are HIV
> positive and people with AIDS;
> the social worker, the volunteer;
> those who work the hot lines,
>> the buddy, the dancer;
> the rabbi, the priest, the pastor;
> the nurse, the doctor, the research technician;
> those who give time, talent, and money;
> those who give love, peace;
> and those who share their life.

We remember them all, God.
> Those with us, those who have died;
> those who are living anonymously and alone,
>> afraid;
> those who have risked all by coming out
>> with their disease;
> those who have been accepted,
>> and those who have not;
> those who work in the agencies and hospitals.

We remember them all, God;
> those who face death and dying,
> and life and living, every day.

We remember them and their strength of spirit
> in the face of AIDS,
> and we remember their zest for life.

Yet, God, we remember the intense pain;
the anguish, tears, sadness, depression;
the anger, fear, hate, and confusion.
Times of blaming, denial, despair, and painful acceptance.

So, God, we ask that you remember us, as well.
Those of us left behind . . . to grieve:
the Mother,
    the Father,
        the Lover,
            the Spouse,
                the Child,
                    the Sister,
                        the Brother;
and those of us who are left to carry on the fight against
    AIDS:
the Mother,
    the Father,
        the Lover,
            the Spouse,
                the Child,
                    the Sister,
                      the Brother.

Will Smith

Closing Hasten the day of healing, merciful God, and help us to bind our wounds today. We pray this and all that is in our hearts and minds. Amen.

Will Smith

15

Learning to Communicate

Holy God, we do not always have the right words, the proper gestures, or the best approach to other people. May we learn to communicate our love and hope and, most important, help us to keep trying. Also, may we enjoy a laugh at ourselves when we goof.

Opening

Maybe the real reason we were led
to devote two years of our lives to lay mission work
was to give rural Venezuelans some good laughs.

Psalm

It's beyond me how they managed
        to keep a straight face
with some of the ways we mangled their language
and their customs.

Once, a young doctor never let on
that I made a mistake when I asked
"Are you paid by the toilets (*sanitarios*)?"
instead of
"Are you paid by the health department (*sanidad*)?"

As soon as the words were out, I realized my error,
but he was most gracious, and serious.

Carol Schuck Scheiber
Logos Translators

Many a moon ago, I arrived late one night at our mission post in Central America. The next morning, Sister and I were all set at 6 a.m. to start the outpatient clinic when a call came for Sister to go to the Aldea for a delivery. She asked me if I'd be all right on my own. She knew that because I'd served in India, Africa, and Haiti, tropical medicine shouldn't be a problem, but Spanish might be.

   I assured her that for six weeks prior to my departure, my husband, who speaks many languages fluently, had drilled me in Spanish for two hours a day, and that he thought I should be all right.

Reading

My first patient was a soldier with bloody diarrhea. I thought his problem was most likely to be hookworm. I asked him to produce a stool sample. He couldn't, so I gave him a jar and told him to return when he'd had a BM.

Two minutes later he came back; he wondered how his BM would fit into such a small bottle. I explained to him that all he had to do was take a little branch from a tree and deposit a small amount of his stool in the jar and return with it as soon as possible.

Sister came back from the Aldea, and we worked our way through many patients.

Suddenly we heard a commotion outside. We looked through the window, and there was my soldier patient with six other soldiers who were carrying a tree. On the very tip of the tree was the patient's stool sample, and on top of that was the jar I'd given him.

I had a sneaking suspicion that my Spanish needed some improvement!

Sylvia Keresztes, MD

Hymn

Loving God, Angél
asked me to write a poem to Georgine
for him:

He said
just put something down
on paper
that comes
from your heart.

As he spoke
you could see
the sadness
in his eyes;
you could hear it
in his voice.

Yet through all this,
I felt his longing
to be able
to tell you
just how much
of a difference you made
in his life.

With your compassion
for him
you helped him
get a glimpse
of what
it must be like
to be loved.

He will never be able
to tell you
but his expressions
are those that will remain
vivid in your memory.

His smile is one
that will remain in your heart.

He said
just write something
that comes from your soul.

Therese Boehnlein
Scalabrinian Missionaries in Mexico

Closing

Thank you, gracious God, for human warmth and generous acceptance in our attempts to reach out to one another. Grant that we will always seek to learn the best ways to touch one another through our actions, words, and presence. Amen.

16

Community

Opening

Courteous God, forming community challenges volunteers. We often learn the best and worst about ourselves. Teach us about community, just as you taught your people throughout the ages, especially through Jesus.

Psalm

Here are a few of the observations I've accumulated
from giving nine orientations
and visiting over twenty different communities.
All names have been changed to protect the guilty.

Few people like washing their own dishes.
Even fewer like washing another's dishes.

When new volunteers walk into a house for the first time,
it looks like they are just carrying in their luggage
        with them.
Wrong. They are also bringing in baggage
(usually in the form of parents, siblings,
        heavy expectations,
hidden heartaches, an assortment of faces,
a hunger to be loved, a hope to be linked,
a recent and highly inflammable argument,
and a rich history worth listening to).

The baggage is usually brought in after the luggage,
during the night perhaps. No one knows for sure.
All of a sudden, about a month into community life,
everyone realizes that the house is really crowded,
and they start trying to get their parents to move out,
or someone else's parents.

Everyone has their own side of any story.
Everyone thinks they are right.
Everyone is wrong. (They should consult me first.)

Most communities appreciate a scapegoat.
And there is often one volunteer
whose behavior suggests an effort at that position
        and title.
Let that person have it.

People are primarily responsible
for their own life and relationships.
Staff (surrogate parents?) get blamed at times
for housemates' (siblings'?) behavior.

Staff can help more if
they are honestly informed by the volunteers.
Volunteers are rarely willing to risk this information.
It is often too little, too late.

Some of us spend energy blaming instead of
getting on with our lives, changing ourselves,
or creating within our circumstances.
We get busy being angry
about not getting exactly what we wanted.
(Hey! Who wouldn't be mad?
They promised *The Sound of Music*
then tell you to "Whistle While You Work.")

It takes a few years to reap the harvest
that the volunteering year can produce.

There are many tests of Christian maturity.
In community, some of these are found
        in how one handles
the proverbial toothpaste cap,
varying standards of cleanliness (or lack of them),
honest admittance of uncomfortable feelings
("Yes, John, it really does bother me
the way you floss your teeth at the table"),
making dinner for six when two show up,
sitting through another meeting.

Realizing that
"My grace is sufficient" and
"my power is perfected in weakness"—
are parts of the terrible beauty of coming face-to-face
with one's own immaturity and need for growth.
We grow when we don't confine God
        to the safe world of ideas,
but give God permission to excavate our being.

Sharon May
Marianist Voluntary Service Communities

Reading

I began the year as idealistic as anyone could be. The first year, community just didn't do it right. We didn't have prayer nights, we didn't plan anything, we didn't even have regular community meetings. Maybe the October retreat would help. Maybe the second half of the year would be right. Maybe.

Maybe not. We lost one of our community mates in a tragic car accident. I hadn't even realized community had started, and it had already changed. We spent the rest of the year trying to keep from drowning in the emotions. We didn't choose to live simply. We tried to celebrate life, because it just may not last long. We didn't pray together. In fact, at times, we didn't pray at all. We didn't discuss our pains and sorrows in community. It just wouldn't work.

But we had some great times on the basketball court, the softball field. Then there was always the hot fudge cake at Plenty's. We found acceptance and trust during those times. It was then that we communicated and were one. But back to community?

I decided to try community again. This time my expectations would be more realistic; I would be more flexible. This time I would challenge my community more. Plus, in my next community, maybe there would be someone headstrong and idealistic who would get the rest of the community in line.

We tried prayer nights once a week. We met once a week. We had community outings, meals together, electricity fasts, rice nights. Our prayer nights were more off than on. Community nights weren't always that unifying. Many ideas and plans were never followed through. Am I failing again?

If I merely change my definition of community, I will have passed both years. Community is not how many times you eat and pray together. Community doesn't happen once a week on the assigned night. Community is a process. Outside of the volunteer community, we can choose the people we live and spend time with.

In community, we are thrown together with people we didn't choose. We struggle with the diversity of the group, teach and challenge one another, and struggle to accept and appreciate one another, connecting with people unlike ourselves. If Jesus had traveled in circles of those who accepted him, he would never have been crucified. But who would have heard of him? His connection unified his followers, and it continues to unify us. We are all called to be community, to become unity, to connect in some way to all who enter our life.

So after two years, I haven't failed. What a relief. And I have given up my quest to be the perfect volunteer. I have learned, and I continue on the journey.

Mary Beth Healy
Jesuit Volunteer Corps

Hymn

I made bread today.
In the silence of the rising sun, I made bread.
It reminded me of my becoming
of everyone's becoming
and all that is a part of that becoming.
The patience needed
and the waiting—
as some of the ingredients cooled—
the smell of the yeast
and the different stages in the making of bread,
all so important,
yet very different from the finished product.
As I began to feel
and knead the bread with my hands,
I thought of the hands of those who help knead me.

They are many hands,
yet all are the hands of God.
I identified with the incomplete, gooey-dough stage—
that part that sometimes doesn't look so good
but you know is coming.
I was aware of the commonness among all people
created by God,
all from the same basic recipe and ingredients
yet each so different—
each loaf
each taste
each texture.
We are of the earth
made with the loving hands of a Mother, Father God.
One bread
one body
one Lord.

Geriann Fedorowicz
Jesuit Volunteer Corps

Closing

God who draws us to unity, "the bottom line is celebrating life and celebrating the gift that each person is. Each person that we live with touches our life, or makes us aware of who we are." Give us open minds and generous hearts to build community among ourselves and in our world. Form us as peacemakers, bridge builders—in short, people of community. Amen.

Laura Libertore
Marianist Voluntary Service Communities

17

Miracles

Thank you, creator God, for all the miracles, large and small, that magnify your presence.

The women at the shelter knew I was new,
and one of them enjoyed giving me a hard time about it.

Despite this, we became close friends,
and it was much to my dismay
that I returned to work one afternoon
and discovered she had moved out unexpectedly.

Not getting a chance to say good-bye is a part of the job
I have not become used to.

A few days later, I came across her file.
When women leave the shelter,
they are asked to answer some questions.

In response to "My favorite thing about . . ."
this woman had written "the staff—especially Kelly!"
I didn't know whether to laugh or to cry.
I miss her.

Kelly Smith
Marianist Voluntary Service Communities

I was home all alone, preparing for a class. Someone knocked. I went to the door. A young woman was there with her infant son wrapped in a white flannel sheet. I had seen her at Mass on Sundays, but did not know her. "My baby has diarrhea and vomiting. I took him to the hospital, but the doctor told me it was too late. He was angry and yelled at me for waiting until the last minute. Please baptize my baby, so that he will get better."
    I invited her in and took the baby into my arms. He weighed nothing. His skin was wrinkled and dry, his eyes sunken into their sockets and listless. He was too weak to cry. The mother looked pleadingly at me. "Father is not in. The baptismal waters will heal my baby." "Yes," I said,

"the baptismal waters will heal your baby and prepare him for life everlasting."

We went across the street to the church. I had baptized before when the priest was not in town. After recording the data, the young mother and I baptized the infant son.

The cleansing water of baptism flowed down his head; he tasted the salt and was anointed with the chrism of prophets, kings, and priests. The mother was radiant. She prayed and offered her son to God, knowing the saving power of her Savior more than I. There were just the three of us present . . . and God was there.

Outside the church, we parted with hugs and tears. It always hurt to see the babies die. I had seen so many. Forty percent of the babies in this country die before reaching age five. I went back to my books with a heavy heart.

About four weeks later, I was walking down the street. Someone called me, "Marianita, Marianita!" I turned. It was the young mother, and in her arms was a restless, fussing baby boy. Thin, but now with bright healthy eyes, full of expression and showing intelligence and life.

I couldn't believe it. But deep inside of me I heard, "Be not unbelieving, but believing. . . . See how great her faith is."

Marianne Dunne
Maryknoll Associate Lay Missioner Program

Hymn

Lately I have been blessed
    with a growing consciousness
of God's partnering me.
Still, to walk in this world without power, security,
    or glamour
is to struggle up the sand dunes of my spiritual desert.

And yet there bloom the flowers—
those little bits of God-given color, fragrance, and life
scattered throughout the dry grasses.

Let me name them:
a kind smile from a guest
who is as intimidated by the drop-in center as I am,
getting lost in a good book that has nothing to do
    with homelessness,
getting lost in a good book that does,

sitting on our front porch with the whole crew
    on a still, hot night,
singing all the radical religious songs we know,
catching our dog playing with his food
when he thinks I'm not watching,
phone calls from my little brother,
romance and laughter,
constancy and ice cream.

For these and other flowers in the desert, I thank you,
    God.

Christine M. Silsby
Jesuit Volunteer Corps

Holy Friend, open our eyes to the many miracles that oc-
cur day by day and often in seemingly unlikely places.
May we see them and praise you, God of wonder. Amen.
Alleluia!

Closing

18

Saying Good-bye

Opening

All-wise God, be present with us now as we pray about our parting. Help us to sort through our experiences and feelings to make what sense of them we can, and help us to trust that you are always with us in our joy and grieving.

Psalm

Angél
i know you are sad
to see me go
but i did not come
to say good-bye
i came for you
to know you
so that you
may know yourself
a little better

you are a dreamer
without courage to dream
you are a lover
but you put no faith
in love

what can i do
to help you believe
you are worth it
life is worth it

there is love
hiding inside of you
i've seen it
but i cannot
show it to you
you only need
to believe
it is there

only then
will you find
what you seek
after today

we will lead
separate lives
once again

after today
i will look for you
in the faces of strangers
i will remember
your troubled smile
carry you
in my heart
until we meet again

i did not come
to say good-bye
i came
so that you might find
the courage
to dream
to love.

Georgine Vickerd
Scalabrinian Missionaries in Mexico

Reading

Change happens all the time. July means bringing the experience of service, simplicity, and community living to a close. It means packing up our belongings and our memories and making way for a new group of volunteers. It means letting go and saying good-bye. For some, this good-bye is difficult because, although the year was temporary, it was still very significant. For others, the year's end may be a welcome change, because the year turned out to be an unexpectedly challenging or stretching experience. In either case, it was a full year.

A year when God was present, whether we were in tune or not. A year when God sought our greatest good and called us into deeper relationship. A year when God gifted us with new awarenesses and shattered old images. A year when God helped each of us to personally define simplicity, community, service, peace, justice, friendship, patience, and laughter. So each of us takes the unique experience of this past year and stores it away in the quiet places of who we have now become. We are also part of one another.

What we have gained or lost because of our encounters are the gifts of this closing moment, to be shared and to be cherished. We hope for one another. And we give thanks to God for this most amazing year of shared and grace-filled journeys.

Laura Libertore
Marianist Voluntary Service Communities

Hymn

From Africa's deep dark
 I shall loathe to depart
  its lavender sunrise
   its mists' throbbing heart . . .
    its juju and charms
   pagan rites and repute
    harmattan, golden moon
    its weird drums and flute . . .
     . . . its jagged, volcanic and
      beauteous Kwa Falls
    its potent, wild witchcrafts
      with quaint animal calls . . .
    its mysterious black nights
      filled with effulgent fireflies
        vultures lazily gliding
    its clear, azure skies.
      From horizon to horizon

the whole bush on fire
with the conversation of drums
sizzling higher and higher. . . .
Then, the sudden, equatorial
and violent rains
bending banana trees
on tropical plains.
Its unique Parrot Island
where grows the plantain
and river banks settled
a straw-thatched domain . . .
the long, spindly legs
of adolescent and child
burned black like matchsticks
and racing the wild.
And somewhere in the night
almost drowned, all alone
the voice of the African
in clear, plaintive tone . . .
rises and falls, and then . . .
loses sound
lost in his own land
where strangers abound.
Still, all this beauty
is here on display
and created by God
in such majestic array!
In silence—yet shouting
"How great is God's love
for Africans! The Creator excelled so!"

Emily Kulchsyki
Los Angeles Lay Mission Helpers

Closing

God, source of hope, as we contemplate parting,
we pray:
God, my life, my way, my hope, my *future,*
I never thought of you as my future.
I always worried about my future—
what was I going to do?
It is so nice to think of you as my future,
like I can relax
instead of trying to figure everything out.
We will move on, but remember: you are our hope.
Amen.

Mary Kondrat
Maryknoll Associate Lay Missioner Program

19

Thanksgiving

Opening

Above all, we thank you, Holy Friend. No matter what the traumas and joys of serving you, we hold to the hope that your Reign will come. Then justice and peace will kiss, and the lion will lay down with the lamb.

Psalm

You come to me, God, in the morning in the songs
    of the birds,
and you gently call my name and wake me.
You have blessed me with food and shelter,
none of these have I received on my own.
I eat my breakfast and think of you.

You come to me, God, in the city, so alive,
the number of people coming and going amazes me.
how I love to hear the simple man singing
as he walks or cycles along.

Someone smiles at me whom I do not know,
then I recognize it as your smile, God.
you really are everywhere!

I walk by a man who is blind.
At first I look away and feel angry about his life.
But you are there, God,
and the blind man calls me to look again,
he has no anger about his life, but acceptance,
he has not given up, but moves on with determination.

How many times have I been on a train, God,
when you have come to me with your hand extended?
What you are really begging for is love
    and some respect.
I love the woman begging
as much as I love my own mother,
neither of them do I really know
for all of us truly belong only to God.

I am so happy, God, that you love me
    in so many different ways.
I think I used to be frightened and stubborn

and look the other way and reject you
when you were the most obviously present in my life.

Thank you for letting me be the individual
you have made me
and for loving me in all things.

Laura Thomas
Sisters of Charity of Nazareth Ministry Corps

Break in the Sky
Break in the Pressure
Blue Skies
Heaven Above
Newness, Freshness
Release from Life to New Life

Reading

Mary Kondrat
Maryknoll Associate Lay Missioner Program

Hymn

This day, O God, has been full.
The events were many,
and the moments of prayer have been
obvious and not so obvious.

Now, I come to you
with all these moments in my heart—
I pray for my fears, my joys.

Hear my anguish, hear my need,
and hear my thanksgiving
for the ordinary moments
and the moments of celebration.

"Resurrection" is not a single event
that occurs at one point in time.
It is constant progress.

Each day I can die to my fears,
uncertainties, and confusions,
and each day, if I hope
and ask you to enter my heart,
I can rise again to openness, confidence, trust, and love.

Our humanness was blessed
from the moment of creation.
Christ validated that blessing by walking this earth
and sharing the holy, ordinary moments with us.

Help me, O Creator, to become anew, daily,
and to recognize the blessing of resurrection,
in the sacred—in the simple!

Laura Libertore
Marianist Voluntary Service Communities

Closing

God of all blessings, "the journey has been long and hard, but we haven't given up yet. In fact, as we look back, we see the growth that you have allowed in us, and we thank you. Even on those days when we feel as if no one understands us, we thank you because we know in our heart that you understand us, and in the end, that is what really matters." For all this glorious life, for the gift of service, for our neighbors, for the earth, we give you praise and thanks. Amen. Alleluia!

Patty Grondin
Spiritan Lay Missionaries

20

Reflection: Hope

Opening

You are always with us, God of hope. May we reflect on this story in light of your wisdom.

Reading

Thank you, God, for having allowed me to touch Simiyu's life, and he mine. Thank you for having used my hands to help you work a miracle in his life.

Oh, it was not so noticeable to most—he did not get up from his bed and walk. But then it was not his body that had been crippled. It was his soul. And after four years of daily loving (and stumbling and falling too), I saw Simiyu take a giant step.

When Simiyu came to our high school he was twenty-one, seven years older than the youngest in his class. His clothes shouted "poverty," but he had a dignified, mature bearing and something unreadable in his eyes.

His first English composition revealed his pain, his caution, and his wanting to hope but not daring to. I could hardly believe his brief history, and I didn't want to.

From a polygamous family, Simiyu and his brother, the only boys, were the eldest of seven children born to their mother. Their father had been an alcoholic most of his life, and the few animals left on the farm had been divided up among the sons of his other, favorite wife. He planned to do the same with the land. Thus, Simiyu's mother's family had no inheritance to look forward to.

At age fourteen, Simiyu left elementary school and home, and hired himself out doing odd jobs just to get enough to eat. He slept wherever he could—in the homes where he worked or in the open fields—and he hoped that one day he would have enough money to pay for the national exams at the end of elementary school, without which one had no hope of going to high school. It took Simiyu seven years to earn the money. During some of the many hopeless days and lonely nights, he almost gave up. "Why did they give birth to me if they didn't want me?" he wrote in his essay.

Simiyu never contacted his parents during his years away from home. Why should they know where he was? Hatred for his father burned deep. But at last, he returned home to finish elementary school. He was a survivor, or perhaps a stoic. He knew that he could even take rejection now. His elementary teachers had always encouraged him, and Simiyu wanted to do his last year of school and the exam with their help. In fact, ever eager to learn and act on advice, Simiyu was a joy to teach.

Simiyu lived at home and learned to be silent, obedient, and respectful to his father. But his high school years proved a struggle. His father did not help with his fees, but an uncle, a poor man whose own children were not successful in school, helped Simiyu when he saw his earnestness and talent for academics.

Simiyu often missed school. Sometimes he was "sent" to buy medicine for his aging, ailing father; to call a doctor for his stepsister-in-law, whose husband worked away from home; to take books to his brother at a boarding school; or to inform relatives when his nephew had died. Being "sent" meant spending many hours on a bicycle or walking when the bicycle was needed on the farm. He used to borrow my bike at times. Then at last our bicycle, yours and mine, God, was yours and his, because he needed it more than I.

Simiyu excelled in all subjects except religion. God as Father never clicked with Simiyu, whose own father had never cared. "The Lord is close to the brokenhearted," we read in the Psalms, but Simiyu found that hard to believe.

Over his four years of high school, Simiyu let *me* come very close to him, God. He turned to me when he had no oil in his lamp for night studies and no one to help with money for the bus to take his mother to the doctor when an ankle infection reduced her to walking on her hands and knees. Remember the times when you and I, gracious God, walked ninety minutes to visit Simiyu's home, when we welcomed him countless times into our home, shared bread and tea with him and his brother during school holidays and some special Saturdays. Sometimes I bought the beans or bananas that he struggled to grow after school on his mother's small piece of land. Often I saw his sagging shoulders lifted as he left my home, where you had brought him, God. Some called him my son.

One day, toward the end of his high school career, Simiyu turned in a poem for a contest, and I was amazed at what you, Holy Spirit, had been doing in his heart. The poem was called "Sunrise." It began:

> The sun
> The powerful eye
> That sees everywhere on arrival
> What have you got in store for me?

In the middle of the poem, he wrote about the effort to study, about leaving his house before sunrise each day. But the later stanzas really captivated me:

> After a tiresome day,
> I pack and away I go.
> Where I go is none
> Other than back
> Back home to my loving parents.

Oh sun!
What will I do for them?
Those two people at home
Will I go back
After four years
To face them empty-handed?

No! Not me!
Sun.

And he ends:

The fortune is for the fortunate ones
And why not me?
I hope it will do.
Yes,
The sun will rise tomorrow.

Somewhere along the line, without my noticing, Simiyu's bitterness had gone. Hope had been allowed to enter his heart.

Simiyu's father was dying during Simiyu's final exams. Simiyu didn't really do his best. But when I visited the family's home on Christmas Day, shortly after his father's death, Simiyu was crafting a bed out of wood! He wasn't sure if he would be able to go on for further study, so he and a friend were starting a small workshop with borrowed tools. God, you and I bought him a few tools of his own before I left Kenya.

When Simiyu went to collect some money that I had sent him through his parish priest recently, the priest wrote me that he was "edified" by Simiyu's visit. I knew what he meant. Simiyu had taken a giant step. Really, I should never have been surprised. He had always been a giant. To have been Simiyu's teacher was a joy, my God. Thank you. I still hold much hope for him, his family, and his future. And most of all, I hope that one day he'll know how much you, God, love him and always have.

Marjorie DeAngelis
Lay Missionary for the Dioceses of Eldoret
and Kakamega, Kenya

21

Reflection:
A Friend in Cincinnati

You are with us, Holy Friend. Dwell with us in our reflection. Teach us your holy wisdom.

Opening

I think the stories that we tell are very important. Through these stories, we share with each other, learn, and get an insight into our own heart and into the hearts and minds of those to whom we tell our tales.

Reading

So this is my story about Nelson, a forty-seven-year-old who seemed in every way to be closer to sixty-seven because of the tragic life that he endured and because of his struggles living in the Over-the-Rhine neighborhood in Cincinnati.

Nelson has been a client of the FreeStore where I am now working in my ministry. I had been there only a short time, working as a receptionist at the intake desk, when I began recognizing the faces and names of those who came often to the FreeStore. Nelson was one of those faces and names, even though I had yet to meet or speak with him. Actually, my first encounter with him was a real eye-opener about what working in the inner city with impoverished, disenfranchised, and needy human beings is like.

I was walking down the ramp of our building to go out to lunch. Struggling up the ramp in slow and measured steps came Nelson. He was wearing his normal attire, winter or summer: a cumbersome, full-length, heavy coat; a hat pulled down over his ears; and a scarf around his neck, almost concealing a rosary he wore. As we met halfway down the ramp, I said hello and casually asked him, "How's the weather today?" Nelson bristled, leaned against the wall, looked me in the eyes, and began cursing and yelling at me—letting me know in no uncertain terms that he was not the *X@*+! weather man, and if he was, he wouldn't let me know anyway.

I was stunned! I felt a little sick, my stomach turned, and with my mouth wide open, I continued down the ramp without another word or glance at Nelson, who continued to stumble his way up the ramp. Once over the shock, I began to realize just how naive and insensitive I was to people and to the conditions in which they struggle to survive every day. Here I was greeting Nelson as if we had met on a quiet, quaint, tree-lined street somewhere in the suburbs. How stupid of me to try and relate to Nelson at that level. I deserved to be cursed at, and Nelson had taught me one of my first lessons about life in the inner city.

As time went on, I would see Nelson at the FreeStore and on the streets as I walked to and from the bus stop. Everyone seemed to know him. Everyone also seemed to know that Nelson was not well. His color became more and more yellow, his stomach grew as big as a beach ball, his legs swelled and bulged from his tight trousers. Nelson was a pathetic sight. He was dying from cirrhosis of the liver.

I can't pinpoint the exact day and location when Nelson and I began talking to each other, whether it was on the church steps where I often saw him sitting or in a hallway at work where we could catch a smoke. But we did begin to talk, gradually opening up, risking, sharing some of our life and background with each other. I began to get to know Nelson, not as the "town drunk," but as Nelson the man.

Nelson grew up in upstate New York, where his father was a prominent surgeon. He attended Catholic grade school and high school and went to college for three years. I found him to be intelligent and quick-witted, with a great sense of subtle sarcasm. His wry sense of humor helped to mask his pain and the demon within—alcohol. And so it became typical for us to talk, hug, and visit whenever we saw each other, on the church steps, at work, or just passing in the streets. I gave Nelson my eyeglass cases that he admired; he gave me pieces of penny candy. A relationship was in the making, and there was risk!

One Friday, Nelson's pants were falling down as he came up to me at my desk. A crowd of people needing assistance faced us. Nelson asked if I could help him with his belt. Both of us were then oblivious to all the people in front of us. I got a scissors and, with Nelson's unsteady hand in assistance, I notched a new hole in his belt. His pants were once again secure around his waist. Nelson leaned over and whispered in my ear, "Thank you, Mike."

That was the last time I was ever to see Nelson. On Monday morning, I was told that Nelson had died over the weekend.

A little bit of me died along with Nelson. I cannot get him out of my mind. I was allowed to take time off work to attend the small church service for him. I miss him. I will be forever grateful that for a little while, we got to know each other.

Mike Allison
Marianist Voluntary Service Communities

22

Reflection: My *Comadre*

Opening

Let us remember the holy presence of God as we reflect.

Reading

Our *comadre,* Hortencia Castro, had died a painful death from cancer. It was terribly hot in Yarinacocha, the little mestizo village of the Peruvian Amazon basin where we lived. There was no rain in sight. Perspiration poured down my face, and my cotton clothes clung to me. We were many. People filled the width of the dirt road, and we formed a procession about a block long. A few "gringos," more mestizos, but mostly Shipibo Indians made up the group. We were old people, young adults, teenagers, and little children like Melita, whose small hand I was holding.

Melita is our goddaughter. When José and Hortencia had asked us to be the baptismal sponsors for their daughter, we were honored, but we tried to talk them into picking a Shipibo Catholic family who would always be near to Melita and share in her life in the way that was customary for extended families among the Shipibos. My husband, Noel, and I knew that although we would live and work with the Shipibos for a number of years, we were always "strangers" and "visitors," and that some day we would leave and return to our own people. José's and Hortencia's minds couldn't be changed, so we became the baptismal sponsors of Melita and members of the extended Castro family. We had no idea that in two years Hortencia would be the one leaving us.

Taking turns carrying the coffin down the rutted, red-clay road, we eventually arrived at the cemetery. The men were still digging, so we quietly stood and watched. Then, with ropes at the head and foot of the black wooden box, the coffin was lowered into the grave prepared for Hortencia. She had received the anointing of the sick, but Father Bernardo was unable to attend the funeral. In Spanish, I led the Catholic prayers. Guillermo Arevelo, Catholic and Shipibo *curandero,* led the group in prayers in the Shipibo language and performed some ancient ritual over the grave.

I had been to many Shipibo burials—too many. This was the first one, however, where the spiritual bond of baptism held us in a special relationship. As godparents of Melita, Noel and I were intimate parts of this Shipibo family. He was in Lima at this time, and our daughter, Wanda, was an infant at home. I was alone for a very intimate and wonderful experience with my Shipibo family.

Our *comadre*, Hortencia, had been a wonderful person and an accomplished Shipibo artist. Her family was highly respected. Glorioso, her oldest son, was a member of an important Shipibo political organization. The two younger boys were hard workers and good students. Three-year-old Melita was the only girl. José, the husband, was a quiet man—humble and hardworking. The Shipibos respected him for his justice and honesty. Hortencia had a lot of sisters and a large, but close, extended family. Hortencia was the mother in a Shipibo family in which the men are often away hunting, fishing, or trading. As such, she served as the center of the family—its strength and force. She was also too young to die, even for a Shipibo woman. At the grave, sighs, moans, tears, and wailing made the profound grief tangible.

We threw dirt in the open hole and then put our flowers on the grave. Quietly and slowly, the mourners turned and started drifting down the red-clay road or disappearing into the high brush that surrounded the country cemetery. I put my flowers on the grave and with tears streaming down my cheeks, kissed Melita. Then I put her little hand into her father's strong hand and started my return home.

A woman put her hand on my arm, indicating that I was to stay with the family. I returned to Melita's side and stood there watching. Only the family remained now. One of the sisters and some nieces gathered dried twigs and branches. They piled these on the grave in a stack nearly as tall as I am. Special, fragrant herbs were placed on top. Kerosene was poured on. In silence, José put a match to the pyre. With a swish, tongues of red, white, and orange flames shot into the sky. I felt the intense heat of the fire and, at the same time, a freeing not only of my *comadre's* spirit but of mine as well.

The grave did not trap Hortencia's spirit. It had risen like the flames, and she was one with the universe. Incredible peace filled my soul. My sadness turned to joy, and I experienced the Resurrection of Jesus and Hortencia. I knew that she would be with us at all times, even to the ends of the earth. She lived in the fragrance of the herbs that had gone up in the smoke and in the fire that had become one with the tropical heat. We silently turned and walked away. No words were necessary.

Walking down the familiar road alone, I thanked God for permitting me to be present for this sacred and ancient ritual. I thanked God for the living experience of the dead. Long before Christians had arrived, these people had understood the relationship between Creator and creature. These wonderful Shipibo people understood this relationship better than those who came to teach them about Jesus, the son of the Creator. Their symbolism and rituals were both explicit and meaningful. I had just experienced a sacramental presence of God.

I thank God for this privilege and now walk more humbly alongside all native peoples, open to the God of creation that they can reveal to me and to all of us.

Because of this experience with the Shipibos and the faith that they have shared with me, I feel the presence of all the people that I have loved and who have died before me. Their presence can be felt in the heat of the day, in the gentle kiss of the breeze, in the smell of incense, and in the colors of a flame.

Marianne Dunne
Lay Missionaries in Peru

23

Reflection: More Adjustments

Merciful God, we rest in your presence. Be in our hearts as we reflect.

Opening

After some of our Venezuelan friends felt close enough to us to be up-front, they joked with us about the crazy way we acted when Matt got sick. Now, Michigan and Indiana natives would probably back us up that the logical way to be when you're sick is *alone*. Sure, someone can be around to fix meals and fetch medicine, but who wants their friends stopping by when they feel feverish and nauseated?

Reading

During our first months in town, Matt came down with a fierce flu. As the town missionaries, we often received visits from both children and adults, but this day he felt too sick to see anyone. I turned away all visitors, assuring them that Matt wasn't up to having company.

What we hadn't realized was that townspeople were coming by precisely *because* Matt was sick. It was their way of showing concern and support.

Another interesting aspect of Venezuelan culture was the persistence of "old wives' tales"—for lack of a better phrase. These days, we Americans consider ourselves too sophisticated to take seriously our own superstitions. We might take note if a black cat crosses our path, but usually it won't ruin our day.

When I was pregnant with our first child in Venezuela, I was bombarded with folklore about how to determine our baby's sex. In retrospect, I see how much I began to invest in the varied opinions on the gender. Actually, ultrasounds—during which gender can usually be determined—have become fairly common, even among rural Venezuelans. But that still didn't take away the fun of trying to guess. I knew my mom was back in Detroit rooting for us to have a girl, so I thought she'd appreciate it if I could pass on a majority opinion in that favor.

Some looked at my shape and declared: girl. Others asked how soon the baby moved: at four months, okay, it's probably a boy. Boys move around early. (One mother said she could feel her son in the first few weeks!) Did little girls come to me or run back to their mothers? If they ran away, it was because I was carrying a boy.

Still, only one of the many speculators seemed truly convinced of the gender. Isabel was gushy, friendly, and flirtatious. She was dying for me to have a girl. "I know exactly how to tell if it's a boy or girl," she assured me. She wrapped a spoon and a fork in separate towels and had me choose one towel. I chose the fork. "Oh no!" Isabel yelled. "Carol, you're going to have a boy." She was close to tears.

I didn't believe her, especially because my informal poll seemed to lean toward a girl. But I have to admit that when the doctor said to me, "Congratulations, it's a boy," I almost didn't believe *him*. How could all those people who had predicted a girl be so wrong? Isabel and the fork were right after all.

Some Venezuelan customs were hard for us to learn. In fact, our ignorance about the Venezuelan manner of calling someone's attention almost cost us our lives. One day we were driving at a pretty good clip when we spotted a young woman from one of the villages where we worked. She waved furiously at us, flexing her hand up and down at the wrist. We smiled broadly and waved back.

After we had passed her, I had a strange feeling that she wasn't just greeting us. "Hey," I said to Matt, bringing all my cultural sensitivity to bear, "I think maybe she wanted us to stop." He slammed on the brakes and signaled to turn left.

However, we still didn't realize that turn signals don't carry as much weight in Venezuelan driving as an American midwesterner might wish. A huge bus decided that we were moving too slowly and bore down on us with frightening speed, passing us on our left. Luckily, what Matt may have lacked in cultural understanding, he made up for in quick reflexes. He jerked the wheel sharply to the right and, with inches to spare, we were saved!

After two years back in the United States, I still beckon to people with Venezuelan hand signals. But of all the things rural Venezuelans taught me, I think the most valuable was learning what it means to be a minority. Even though I am a white, middle-class North American raised in a Detroit suburb, I know in my heart how it feels to be different. I know how it feels not to fit in, not to agree with the dominant culture's assumptions and customs. I understand a little bit about how new immigrants feel after they get to the United States.

Oftentimes when you don't speak the language, people think less of you no matter how educated or eloquent you might be in your native tongue. When you don't do things the same way as the dominant culture—whether in cooking, dressing, or waving to a friend—you can feel out of step. When you're five feet eleven inches and pale in a society of much shorter, dark-complected men and women, people stare and take note. You can never just blend in visually.

In short, being a minority can be a struggle. But for me, the strain was eased because Venezuelans were so welcoming and accepting. How to accept newcomers and offer friendship and love—that is the greatest thing rural Venezuelans taught this Michigan native.

Carol Schuck Scheiber
Logos Translators

Index

Acknowledgments (*continued*)
All of the scriptural quotations in this book are freely adapted. These adaptations are not to be interpreted or used as official translations of the Scriptures.

The quotation on page 10 is from *Praying Our Experiences,* by Joseph F. Schmidt (Winona, MN: Saint Mary's Press,1989), page 9. Copyright © 1980, 1989 by Saint Mary's Press. All rights reserved.

The excerpts by Laura Thomas on pages 15–16, 33, and 34 originally appeared in the February 1992 issue of *SC News,* a newsletter published by the Sisters of Charity of Nazareth. Used by permission of the Sisters of Charity of Nazareth congregation.

The excerpt by Carol Schuck Scheiber on page 29 originally appeared in "What We Brought Back from Venezuela," *Salt* magazine (May 1990), pages 18–23. Reprinted with permission from *Salt* magazine. Published by Claretian Publications, 205 West Monroe, Chicago, IL 60606.

The excerpt by Carol Schuck Scheiber on pages 43–44 originally appeared in *P.I.M.E. World Magazine.* Used with permission.

The excerpt by Dr. Sylvia Keresztes on pages 61–62 is reprinted from "Just Following Orders," *Punch Digest for Canadian Doctors,* page 10. Used with permission of *Punch Digest for Canadian Doctors.*

Photo credits: Mary Farrell, cover; Jean-Claude Lejeune, cover (lower right); The Crosiers/Catholic News Service, page 14; Mimi Forsyth/Catholic News Service, page 39; KNA/Catholic News Service, page 88; Jean-Claude Lejeune, pages 31, 34, 41, 51, 67, 71, 73, 77, 80, 90; Fabvienen Taylor/Catholic News Service, page 60; UPI/Bettman, pages 23, 84